J
796.332 Aaseng, Nathan
Aa   Football's Super
          Bowl champions, IX
          XVI

DATE DUE

AG 6 '85	AP 1 3 '89	JA 2 8 '92	JY 2 3 '04
AG 19 '85	SE 1 9 '89	FE 5 '92	DE 02 '08
SE 4 '85	NO 2 4 '89	FE 1 9 '92	AG 1 6 '72
NO 5 '86	JA 4 '90	MR 3 0 '92	MR 0 3 '72
JA 22 '87	JA 2 3 '90	JY 1 6 '92	JY 0 5 '79
DE 9 '87	MY 2 '90	JAN 1 0 '95	
MR 1 2 '88	JY 1 2 '90	AUG 0 4 '95	
JY 0 7 '88	NO 2 6 '90	JUN 2 3 '97	
AG 2 0 '88	DE 1 2 '90	JUL 0 9 '97	
NO 2 2 '88	MY 2 8 '91	JAN 0 4 '99	
NO 2 6 '88	NO 1 '91	AG 2 5 '99	
FE 6 '89	NO 1 4 '91	MR 1 4 '00	

The SPORTS HEROES Library

Football's SUPER BOWL CHAMPIONS IX-XVI

Nathan Aaseng

Lerner Publications Company • Minneapolis

ACKNOWLEDGMENTS: The photographs are reproduced through the courtesy of: pp. 4, 6, 10, 24, 28, 30, 32, 55, 57, 63, 64, 67, 68, 72, 76, 77, Wide World Photos, Inc.; p. 8 (left), Green Bay Packers; pp. 8 (right), 61, Dallas Cowboys; pp. 13, 14, 15, 31, Pittsburgh Steelers; pp. 18, 20, 22, 25, 33, 39, 40, 42, 47, 50, 54, 56, 58, 65, 66, 73, 74, 78, Vernon J. Biever; p. 48, John E. Biever; p. 37, Los Angeles Rams; p. 71, San Francisco 49ers. Cover photograph by Vernon J. Biever.

To David Linné

LIBRARY OF CONGRESS CATALOGING IN PUBLICATION DATA

Aaseng, Nathan.
   Football's Super Bowl champions, IX-XVI.

   (The Sports heroes library)
   Continues: Football's Super Bowl champions.
   Summary: Describes the winning performances of the
Pittsburgh Steelers, Oakland Raiders, Dallas
Cowboys, and San Francisco Forty-niners in their
Super Bowl victories from 1975 through 1982.
   1. Super Bowl Game (Football)—History—Juvenile
literature. 2. Football players—United States—
Biography—Juvenile literature. [1. Super Bowl
Game (Football)—History. 2. Football—History]
I. Title. II. Series.
GV956.2.S8A19   796.332'7   82-10099
ISBN 0-8225-1333-1

Manufactured in the United States of America

International Standard Book Number: 0-8225-1333-1
Library of Congress Catalog Card Number: 82-10099

3 4 5 6 7 8 9 10 92 91 90 89 88 87 86 85 84

Contents

Cowboys Randy White (54), Harvey Martin (79), and Ed "Too Tall" Jones (72) tighten the noose around Bronco quarterback Craig Morton in Super Bowl XII action.

Introduction

Perhaps the era of the super team in pro football ended in the 1980s. By then such unstoppable powers as the Miami Dolphins of the early 1970s and the Pittsburgh Steelers of the late 1970s had been replaced by a balanced league. National Football League officials were fond of saying that on any given Sunday, any pro team was capable of beating any other. Teams that had been shrugged off as losers fought their way to the championship.

But even with a balanced league, the Super Bowl still holds its drama and excitement. Not only is it the biggest single sporting event in the country, it has also grown into a weeklong party and spectacle. National television and newspapers scramble for every bit of news they can get, and players are still in demand every spare minute before the game. At stake is the championship of pro football, and winning it takes as much talent and courage as ever.

On a chilly Sunday in New Orleans, thousands of Super Bowl IX fans pack Tulane Stadium before the Vikings-Steelers championship game.

Many great players and fine teams have never reached that goal. The Minnesota Vikings, Philadelphia Eagles, San Diego Chargers, and Houston Oilers have all fielded excellent teams that have fallen short. Why have they failed while others have succeeded? What does it take to be a Super Bowl champion?

There have been many attempts to pin down the reasons why a team wins or loses the Super Bowl. Whenever a tightly disciplined team loses the game, some analysts say their coach was too strict. And

6

when a more loose-knit group loses, they say he wasn't strict enough. Yet both the no-nonsense Green Bay Packers and the wilder Oakland Raiders have won two Super Bowls each.

The fact is, there is no single recipe to follow in trying to put together a Super Bowl winner. Compare the strengths of the Super Bowl champions in this book:

Pittsburgh Steelers: big-play offense, aggressive defense

Dallas Cowboys: deceptive offense, disciplined defense

Oakland Raiders: varied offense, freelancing defense

San Francisco 49ers: trick-play offense, big-play defense

These teams prove that there's no pattern to what goes into the making of a Super Bowl champion.

Is it then just a matter of having the best players? Not according to some of the more recent Super Bowls. When judged on talent alone, neither the 1980 Oakland Raiders nor the 1981 San Francisco 49ers rated much above average. Neither were

Two quarterbacks who led their teams to a pair of Super Bowl victories: Bart Starr (left) of the Green Bay Packers and Roger Staubach of the Dallas Cowboys.

considered to have even enough talent to challenge for their divisional title, much less a Super Bowl.

If you look at who has won the Most Valuable Player Award in Super Bowls, however, it appears that there finally may be a clue to what makes a Super Bowl winner. Nine of the 16 MVPs have been quarterbacks. Could it be that the quarterback is the key? Quarterbacks happen to play the most noticeable position and are, therefore, the most likely candidates for the award when no one player stands out. But even in games in which a quarterback has won the MVP, such things as a key pass catch, fine blocks, interceptions, referees' decisions, fumbles, kicks, or just plain luck have often had a much greater role in determining the winner.

So what separates a Super Bowl champion from the rest of the field? Just one thing. When it comes down to the day of the game, the winning team is able to do its job well, despite being faced with tremendous pressure. This book shows how the Super Bowl champions, starting with the Pittsburgh Steelers, have been able to make their mark when it counted most. These are the ones who have survived the tension. They are the Super Bowl champions.

Leaving himself dangerously unprotected, Lynn Swann leaps high in the air to catch a Super Bowl XIV pass. Ram defender Pat Thomas made the tackle but arrived too late to stop another Steeler gain.

1
Pittsburgh Steelers

SUPER BOWL IX
SUPER BOWL X
SUPER BOWL XIII
SUPER BOWL XIV

While the Super Bowl pressure caused a lot of shakiness on the field over the years, it only seemed to bring out the best in the Pittsburgh Steelers. Without a doubt, Pittsburgh has been the top Super Bowl team of all time. They treated the game as their own personal showcase, and they won all four Super Bowls in which they played.

Ten years ago, the Steelers would have been the last team anyone expected to dominate pro football. The team was bought by Art Rooney for $2,500 back in 1933. And for most of their history, the Steelers played as though they weren't worth any more. In 1969 Chuck Noll arrived to coach a team that had managed only 8 winning seasons in their 36-year history.

At first it seemed that Noll would continue the poor Steeler tradition. After winning the season opener in 1969, his team lost 16 games in a row over two seasons. But Noll was patiently building a team through the college draft. It would become a Noll trademark to have a squad made up only of players he had drafted or signed as free agents and no trades.

Noll gradually formed his team in a series of six drafts and got the following players:

1969: Joe Greene (defensive tackle), L.C. Greenwood (defensive end), Jon Kolb (offensive tackle)
1970: Terry Bradshaw (quarterback), Mel Blount (cornerback)
1971: Jack Ham (linebacker), Dwight White and Ernie Holmes (defensive linemen),

Coach Chuck Noll (right) and Terry Bradshaw, the architect and the builder of Pittsburgh's four Super Bowl championships, talk over their plans on the sidelines.

Mike Wagner (safety), Larry Brown (tight end), Gerry Mullins (guard)

1972: Franco Harris (fullback), Steve Furness (defensive lineman)

1973: J.T. Thomas (cornerback)

1974: Lynn Swann and John Stallworth (wide receivers), Mike Webster (center), Jack Lambert (linebacker), Donnie Shell (safety), Randy Grossman (tight end)

13

L.C. Greenwood (Arkansas AM&N)

Jack Lambert (Kent State)

John Stallworth (Alabama A&M)

Franco Harris (Penn State)

14

Joe Greene (North Texas State)

Lynn Swann (USC)

Mel Blount (Southern)

Jack Ham (Penn State)

Twelve All-Pro players emerged from that roster. When they were added to veteran linebacker Andy Russell, the Steelers had the makings of an excellent team.

The Steelers' defense developed more quickly than their offense. By 1974 the defensive line stopped offenses so easily that it became known as the "Steel Curtain." Some of football's finest offensive units bounced off the Steel Curtain in the 1974 play-offs without making a dent. The Steelers bottled up Buffalo's great runner, O.J. Simpson, in a 32-14 triumph. Then they buried Oakland's huge blockers and allowed the Raiders only 29 yards running in a 24-13 victory.

Before the January 12, 1975, Super Bowl in New Orleans, defensive end Dwight White became so ill that he was forced to stay in a hospital. But he checked out the day before the game, determined to play against the Minnesota Vikings. Because of the work of White and his mates, the Vikings' running game could easily have taken White's place in the hospital! Tackles Joe Greene and Ernie Holmes overwhelmed their opponents, and Minnesota managed a total of only 17 yards in 21 carries.

With the Viking running game stopped in its

tracks, the Vikings' only hope was to pass. Minnesota blockers fought off the Pittsburgh rush, keeping quarterback Fran Tarkenton from being sacked. The long arms of 6-foot, 6-inch Steeler end L.C. Greenwood, however, kept knocking down passes. Tarkenton saw four of his tosses whacked to the ground by Greenwood and company.

Only an equally fine performance by the Viking defense kept the game close in the first half. In fact, the only points scored by either side in the first 30 minutes belonged to the Steeler defense. Facing a second down and seven situation at their own 10-yard line, the Vikings fumbled a handoff. The ball bounced backward, Tarkenton fell on it, and Dwight White downed him. Since Tarkenton had slid into the end zone, the Steelers were awarded two points for a safety.

Near the end of the half, Minnesota threatened to take the lead. Tarkenton fired a ball down the middle of the field to John Gilliam, who was open near the Pittsburgh goal line. But just as Gilliam grabbed the ball, he was blasted by Steeler safety Glen Edwards. The ball popped up, and Mel Blount intercepted to end the drive.

In the second half, a bad break turned out to be a good break for Pittsburgh. Roy Gerela slipped as

It's two points for the Steelers as they cover Fran Tarkenton in the Viking end zone for a safety and the lead in Super Bowl IX.

he kicked off, and the ball only traveled a short way. Viking Bill Brown, however, could not pick the ball off the ground, and the Steelers recovered at the Viking 30. The Pittsburgh offense took over, wearing new shoes that helped them to get their footing on the slippery artificial turf. (For just such an occasion, their equipment manager had bought shoes from Canada that were not even on the market yet.) Pittsburgh drove the 30 yards for the score with Franco Harris getting the touchdown. Minnesota botched other chances to get back in the game by missing field goals and by fumbling on Pittsburgh's five-yard line.

In the fourth quarter, the Viking defense got a score for their team when Matt Blair broke through to block Bobby Walden's punt. Viking Terry Brown pounced on it in the end zone for six points. But the Vikings missed the extra point, and the Steelers still led by three.

Pittsburgh's offense chose this time to produce the only successful long drive of the game. Most of the yards in the game came on trap plays to Franco Harris, who would run to his left and wait to see which way the linemen blocked the Vikings. Then he would slip through for a good gain.

The Steelers drove toward the Viking end zone and then tried one of their few passes in the game. Quarterback Terry Bradshaw passed to tight end Larry Brown, who gained 30 yards before losing control of the ball. The Vikings recovered, thinking they now had a chance to start their own game-winning drive. But the officials ruled that Brown was down before he fumbled. So Pittsburgh kept the ball and scored on a seven-yard pass to Brown.

The Vikings didn't come close to scoring, and what was possibly the worst Super Bowl ever ended 16-6 in favor of Pittsburgh.

Steeler blockers hold off Minnesota's All-Pro tackle Alan Page long enough for Franco Harris to find running room. Harris' 158 yards rushing against a good Minnesota defense set a Super Bowl record.

If they could have given a Most Valuable Player Award to an entire defense, the Steel Curtain would have been most deserving. But that afternoon the award went to the only offensive player to find success—Franco Harris. Harris had broken Larry Csonka's Super Bowl rushing record by gaining 158 yards on 34 carries.

Again a Super Bowl had been fairly dull and sloppily played. Even the most enthusiastic fans had to admit that Super Bowls had become disappointing. That changed the next season, however, when the Steelers returned to face the miracle Cowboys from Dallas. The Cowboys had survived the play-offs on a desperate "Hail Mary" pass from Roger Staubach to Drew Pearson that had taken them 50 yards in the final seconds. Dallas was an exciting, young team and likely to try anything in an attempt to beat the mighty Steelers.

From the very first play, fans knew that this Super Bowl would be different. Dallas took the kickoff and ran a fancy reverse to Thomas Henderson, who ran in the opposite direction of the blockers. By the time the Steelers put on the brakes and doubled back to catch him, Henderson had returned the kick for 48 yards. Neither team, however, could score in their first offensive possession, and Pittsburgh's Bobby Walden prepared to punt back to Dallas. He could not hold on to the snap from center, though, and Dallas took over on the Steeler 27. Before Pittsburgh could catch its breath from running on the field, Dallas scored on a pass to Pearson who was wide open in the middle of the field.

Franco Harris found the going tough, but the Steelers had developed a new weapon over the past

Steeler fullback Franco Harris grinds out tough yards against the Cowboys in Super Bowl X.

year. Lynn Swann, who had been hurt so badly in the play-offs that he did not know if he could play against Dallas, came up with remarkable plays. And although Cowboy cornerback Mark Washington stayed with him like a magnet, Swann still came down with important catches. His 32-yard grab set up a short scoring pass to tight end Randy Grossman. After a Cowboy field goal made it 10 to 7 in favor of Dallas, he made an incredible 52-yard catch while sprawling over a falling Cowboy defender. This catch, however, was wasted when Pittsburgh missed a field goal.

The 10 to 7 halftime score held up until the fourth period. Then the Steeler defense, which had become so powerful that their roster was practically an All-Star listing, shut down the Cowboy offense. All-Pros L.C. Greenwood and Dwight White wrecked Dallas' shotgun passing formation, throwing Roger Staubach for losses seven times! The other All-Pros—tackle Joe Greene, linebackers Andy Russell, Jack Ham, and Jack Lambert, and cornerback Mel Blount—joined in stopping the Cowboy running attack.

In the fourth quarter, Pittsburgh eked out a narrow 12 to 10 lead on a safety, by blocking a punt out of the end zone, and with a field goal. Then Mike Wagner, one of the few Steeler defenders who was not voted All-Pro, intercepted Roger Staubach and returned the ball to the Cowboy 7. But Pittsburgh could not get across the goal line, and they had to settle for a 15-10 lead on another Roy Gerela field goal.

Although Steeler kicker Roy Gerela missed this second quarter field-goal attempt, his 36-yard three pointer in the fourth quarter of Super Bowl X gave Pittsburgh the lead. Gerela later booted an 18-yard field goal.

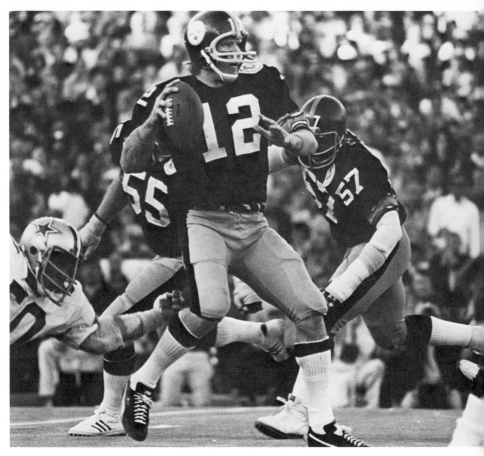

Terry Bradshaw eyes a Steeler target as he moves to avoid the Cowboy rush.

Minutes later Pittsburgh had the ball again and was facing a third and four on their 36-yard line. They did not want to give the ball back to the Cowboys, who were just a touchdown from winning the ballgame. Terry Bradshaw called for a long pass, hoping that the Cowboys would be expecting a short one. As he dropped back to pass, the

25

Cowboys sent their linebackers and even a safety, Cliff Harris, on a blitz. Just before he was jolted by Harris, Bradshaw ducked away from Cowboy D.D. Lewis and threw the ball as hard as he could. Bradshaw was knocked dizzy and never saw the end of the play. He missed the excitement of seeing Swann gracefully gather in the pass 70 yards away and glide into the end zone for a touchdown.

Dallas came back to score quickly on a long pass to Percy Howard and then, thanks to questionable Steeler strategy, they had a chance for an upset. The Steelers ran the ball on fourth down near midfield, hoping to run some time off the clock. They failed, however, to get the first down. And according the NFL rules, the clock stopped whenever the ball went over to the other team. That gave Dallas the ball in good field position with 1:22 left in the game. They made Steeler fans nervous by getting to Pittsburgh's 38, but they failed on their last three passes. Pittsburgh had won again, 21 to 17.

This time it did not take a football expert to know who deserved the Most Valuable Player Award. Lynn Swann, with four splendid catches for 161 yards, had won the game for Pittsburgh.

The next two years, Pittsburgh was knocked out of the play-offs by Oakland and Denver. Their defense, while still tough, was starting to slow down, and their linemen no longer manhandled their opponents. But by this time, the Steeler offense had changed from a fairly ordinary ball-control team to a high-scoring unit that could score from anywhere on the field. Wide receiver John Stallworth joined Swann to give them the league's finest pair of wide receivers. And Terry Bradshaw had gained the experience to make him the top quarterback in the game. The Steeler offensive line had literally grown from an average bunch to a unit that could have passed for an Olympic weight-lifting team! Led by burly center Mike Webster, they gave Bradshaw time to wait until a receiver got open. And when Pittsburgh needed the tough yards, they could still count on the steady running of Franco Harris and Rocky Bleier.

This team thrashed the Houston Oilers, 34-5, on an icy field to win a Super Bowl spot in 1979. Their old rival, the Cowboys, had beaten Los Angeles just as easily, 28-0, to gain a chance for revenge on Pittsburgh. Both teams appeared to be so strong that the game of January 21, 1979, was advertised as the best Super Bowl match ever.

In Super Bowl XIII, Cowboy running back Tony Dorsett galloped for 96 yards in 15 carries.

As always the Cowboys started fast. Speedy half-back Tony Dorsett ran one play to the left, one straight ahead, and one to the right on the Orange Bowl grass in Miami. Each play worked as he raced for 38 yards on three carries. Dallas, however, tried to get a little too clever. With first down on Pittsburgh's 34, they sent Drew Pearson circling around on a flanker reverse. Pearson could not control the handoff, and Steeler John Banaszak recovered the ball at the 47. A few passes advanced the ball to the 28, and then Bradshaw found Stallworth in the end zone for a score and a 7-0 lead.

Dallas started another drive, running surprisingly well against the Steelers. But after reaching the Steeler 39, they went to the pass. Steve Furness caught Staubach for a 7-yard loss, followed by a Dwight White sack for another 10-yard loss that killed the drive.

Near the end of the quarter, Cowboy end Harvey Martin threw aside his opponent and got to Bradshaw before he could throw. Terry dropped the ball and Dallas' Ed Jones recovered on the Pittsburgh 41. On the third down play, Staubach threw to Tony Hill at the 26. Hill raced down the sidelines past Pittsburgh's Blount, who was so busy watching Drew Pearson that he did not see Hill. The play was good for a touchdown and a tie game.

Franco Harris could not find any room to run, so the Steelers were forced into passing situations. On a third and 10, Bradshaw bobbled the ball, and when he tried to control it and run to the outside, he was grabbed by linebacker Thomas Henderson. While Henderson had Bradshaw's arms pinned, Cowboy Mike Hegman pulled the ball away and ran untouched to the end zone, 37 yards away. Dallas 14, Pittsburgh 7.

Three Cowboys arrive too late to stop Pittsburgh's John Stallworth from scoring the first Steeler touchdown on a 28-yard pass from Terry Bradshaw.

Again Dallas forced the Steelers into a third down play deep in the Steeler end of the field. They may have been better off letting Pittsburgh gain yards running the ball. Bradshaw threw to Stallworth for first-down yardage, but the tall receiver was not satisfied with that. He faked out a Cowboy defender and broke into the clear. No one could catch the speedy Stallworth as he dashed 75 yards for the tying touchdown.

Before halftime, Mel Blount stopped another Cowboy drive with an interception, and Pittsburgh had a chance to grab the lead. Helped by a 29-yard catch by Swann, the Steelers moved to the Dallas 7. Bradshaw rolled to his right and threw a high pass toward Rocky Bleier. The veteran running back went high to grab it and held on for the touchdown.

Pittsburgh veteran Rocky Bleier made only one catch in Super Bowl XIII, but it counted for seven yards, a touchdown, and the lead—a lead that the Steelers would hold for the rest of the game.

Longtime standout Jackie Smith clenches his fists in frustration after dropping a sure touchdown pass from Roger Staubach. Smith's blunder cost Dallas a chance to tie the game.

Then Dallas had a perfect chance to even the score in the third period. They drove to the Pittsburgh 10, where they faced a third and 3. The Steelers sent in a blitz against Staubach, but Roger quickly spotted veteran tight end Jackie Smith unguarded in the end zone. It was too easy for Staubach to believe. He threw the ball a little too softly, slightly behind Smith. As the ball floated toward him, Smith reached back slightly to make the catch. He slipped as he did so and stunned himself and the Cowboy fans by dropping the ball. Dallas settled for a field goal and a 21-17 score.

In the fourth quarter, the Steelers took advantage of a series of breaks to pull away from the Cowboys. First Lynn Swann got his legs tangled with those of defender Bennie Barnes on a long pass. Barnes was certain that Swann would be called for interfering on the play. The Cowboys were shocked when the official called Barnes for interference

A major reason for Pittsburgh's 35 points in Super Bowl XIII was their muscular offensive line.

instead! The official's decision cost the Cowboys 33 yards. The Steelers then sent Franco Harris straight ahead from the 23-yard line. After he broke through the line of scrimmage, there was only one Cowboy in position to make the tackle— safety Charlie Waters. Waters, unfortunately, was cut off by an official who happened to be in the way. Harris ran untouched for a score that made it 28 to 17.

On the next kickoff, Cowboy Randy White tried to field a short kick, even though he was wearing a cast on a broken arm. He couldn't come up with the ball, and Pittsburgh's Dirt Winston recovered on the 18. One play later, Swann soared high above the end zone to gather in a scoring pass for a 35-17 lead.

Dallas roared back with two touchdowns in the final minutes on the running of Dorsett and the passing of Staubach. But the rally fell just short as Steeler Rocky Bleier recovered Dallas' final on-side kick. Pittsburgh won, 35 to 31, and Terry Bradshaw had the good fortune to be in the Super Bowl when he played his best game ever. He had completed 17 of 30 passes for 318 yards and four touchdowns to provide the points for his team. For his efforts, he was voted the Most Valuable Player.

Super Bowl XIII MVP Terry Bradshaw dodges Cowboy Ed "Too Tall" Jones.

By the next season, people expected Pittsburgh to keep winning Super Bowls. Again they swept through the AFC play-offs, polishing off Houston, 27-14, for the championship. The best the NFC could put up against them were the Los Angeles Rams. The Rams' 9-7 regular season record was the worst of any Super Bowl contestant, and they were thought to be no match for Pittsburgh.

But on January 20, 1980, in Pasadena, the Rams, always a powerful defensive team, came out fighting. After Pittsburgh took the lead on a 41-yard Matt Bahr field goal, the Ram offense started to move. Few experts thought the Rams could run against the Steelers. The Jack Lambert-led defense had held two strong running teams, Miami and Houston, to a total of 49 yards in the two play-off games. The Rams' Wendell Tyler, however, made almost that much in one first-quarter play. He dodged two Steelers at the line of scrimmage, faked out two more downfield, and scampered for 39 yards. This set up 240-pound Cullen Bryant for a 1-yard touchdown run.

Fortunately for the Steelers, their kickoff returner, Larry Anderson, was ripping through the Rams' special teams. His returns of 45, 38, 32, and 37 yards gave his team fine field position at a time when the Rams were outplaying them. The Steelers used this field position to launch a short drive that ended with a 1-yard end sweep by Harris for a 10-7 lead.

Los Angeles came back under the direction of inexperienced quarterback Vince Ferragamo. As he moved his team with accurate passing, the youngster did not seem to notice the pressure of the Super Bowl or the Steelers. The Rams went into halftime with a 13-10 lead after field goals of 31 and 45 yards by Frank Corral.

In 1978 Los Angeles kicker Frank Corral booted 31 extra points and 29 field goals. His 118 total points led the NFL.

But despite the close score, things did not look good for Pittsburgh. Franco Harris simply could not move the ball against Jack Youngblood, Larry Brooks, and company. Meanwhile the Rams showed they could run on the Steelers.

But the Steelers had so many weapons that when most of them failed, there was always another one waiting to be used. In the second half, they went for the big play with Swann and Stallworth. First it was Swann sprinting past the Ram defenders. Bradshaw threw the ball just past the fingertips of safety Nolan Cromwell, and Swann took it in for a 47-yard touchdown.

Los Angeles decided to show the Steelers they could do the same type of thing. Billy Waddy grabbed a pass good for 50 yards. The Steelers were caught off guard when halfback Lawrence McCutcheon started off on what looked like one of the Rams' favorite plays, an end sweep. Suddenly McCutcheon pulled up and threw to Ron Smith, who was unnoticed in the end zone, for a score and a 19-17 lead.

The Rams now had a chance to stretch their lead. Bradshaw tried a pass over the middle, but Nolan Cromwell swooped in to intercept. Had he hung on to the ball, it would have been a sure touchdown. But the ball fell to the ground for an incomplete pass.

In the fourth quarter, the Steelers knew they needed another big play. The Rams continued to stop their running, and Pittsburgh faced a third and seven on their own 28. Bradshaw called a play that the Steelers had worked on while practicing for the Super Bowl. The play, however, called a "Prevent

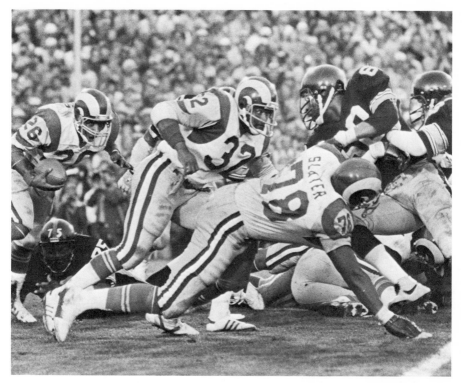
Wendell Tyler breaks through the grasp of "Mean" Joe Greene and follows running mate Cullen Bryant into the Steeler line.

Slot, Hook and Go," had never worked in practice. But this time John Stallworth raced downfield past the Rams' Rod Perry. Perry was supposed to have help from another defensive back, but the man forgot his assignment. Bradshaw fired a perfect pass that Stallworth caught in full stride. And Stallworth raced 73 yards for a 24-19 lead!

Next, two more big plays sealed the victory for the Steelers. First Jack Lambert intercepted a Ram pass on his own 14-yard line to stop a drive.

Steeler linebacker Jack Lambert tucks away a big interception in
Super Bowl XIV.

Then, looking back over his head, Stallworth came up with an incredible catch. The play was good for 45 yards, and it helped the Steelers score a final Franco Harris touchdown.

The inspired play of the Rams had helped make the game a truly memorable Super Bowl. So did the play of the Steeler stars who somehow came up with a remarkable performance whenever their team needed it the most. Jack Lambert had made 14 tackles as well as his key interceptions. Larry Anderson had gained 158 yards on five kickoff returns. Many thought that John Stallworth should have been voted the Most Valuable Player for his acrobatic catches. But that award again went to quarterback Terry Bradshaw who had played flawlessly in the fourth quarter after a rough start. After four Super Bowl wins in four tries, the Steelers truly deserved to be called the greatest Super Bowl team of all time.

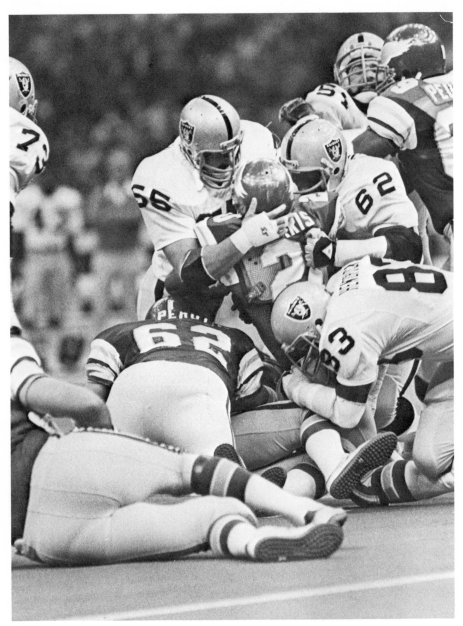

The Raiders crush Eagle running back Leroy Harris in Super Bowl XV.

2
Oakland Raiders

SUPER BOWL XI
SUPER BOWL XV

The Oakland Raiders have always enjoyed their reputation as the free-thinking, hard-hitting outlaws of professional football. Owner Al Davis has run the club in his own mysterious way—a way that often left his fellow NFL club owners puzzled. He welcomed problem players—men with great talent but who did not get along well with coaches or players. The best example of this was giant defensive end John Matuszak. Matuszak had been the first player chosen in the 1973 draft, but he had been cut or traded by frustrated coaches in Houston, Kansas City, and Washington.

Davis had astounded the experts by using his first draft choice in 1973 to draft a punter, Ray Guy of Mississippi State. Other teams did not bother looking for a punter until the later rounds of the draft. Davis also crossed up opponents by using left-handed quarterback Kenny Stabler and running plays to the left more than to the right.

The Raiders also played a rough brand of football that did not win them friends around the league. Hard hits by defensive backs George Atkinson and Jack Tatum sparked a series of fines and law suits.

Oakland also had a reputation that they did not care to have. More than any other team in football, the Raiders were the team that had always lost the big games. Despite having the best record in football throughout the late 1960s and the 1970s, Oakland had appeared in only one Super Bowl. And then they had lost badly. Since that 1968 defeat at the hands of the Green Bay Packers, the Raiders had made it to the final round of the play-offs six out of eight years. But they had lost every time. The Jets had beat them, 27-23, in 1968, and Kansas City won the next year, 17-7. The Raiders had lost to Baltimore, 27-17, in 1970; to Miami, 27-10, in 1973; and to Pittsburgh twice—24-13 in 1974 and 16-10 in 1975.

In 1976 it seemed as though the Raiders had a great chance to avoid playing the powerful Steelers in the play-offs. The Steelers had started slowly that year and had trailed Cincinnati in their divisional race. Late in the season, Cincinnati had played at Oakland. By then the Raiders had already won their division, and they had no reason to play hard against the Bengals. And Oakland knew that if the Bengals won, they would knock the powerful Steelers out of the play-offs.

But Oakland did not want to take the easy way out. They thrashed the Bengals and set up a match with Pittsburgh for the championship of the AFC. In that game, Pittsburgh played without running backs Franco Harris and Rocky Bleier, who had been injured in their play-off win over the Baltimore Colts. But the Steelers probably could not have won even if they had played. Oakland mowed down a healthy Steeler defense, gaining 157 yards running and getting the needed passes from quarterback Ken Stabler for a 24-7 win.

On January 9, 1977, in the Super Bowl at Pasadena, California, the Raiders faced another frustrated Super Bowl team—the Vikings. The Vikings were counting on their all-purpose runner Chuck Foreman and the throws of crafty Fran

Tarkenton to Ahmad Rashad and Sammy White to win their first Super Bowl in four tries.

Early in the game, the breaks seemed to be going against Oakland. They drove downfield into Viking territory, only to miss a field goal from the 29. Then for the first time in his pro career, star punter Ray Guy had a punt blocked. Viking linebacker Fred McNeil raced in from the side and swatted the ball back toward the goal line. McNeil fell on the ball at the Raider three-yard line.

On the second down from the 2, Minnesota sent running back Brent McClanahan into the right side of the line. Raider linebacker Phil Villapiano slipped past the Viking blockers and jolted the runner into fumbling. Willie Hall recovered for Oakland on the 3.

Three plays later, the Raiders made the key play of the game. Two running plays had been stopped by Minnesota's Jeff Siemon, leaving Oakland with a third and seven on their own 6. If they were forced to punt, which seemed likely, they would give Minnesota good field position again.

The Oakland strategy, however, was "when in need, run left." Two huge All-Pros played on that side of the line—290-pound Art Shell and 265-pound Gene Upshaw. Together they outweighed

Oakland's Clarence Davis, running behind his wall of blockers, found plenty of room to run in Super Bowl XI. He ground out 137 yards and early in the game made a crucial third-down run with Oakland struggling deep in their own territory.

their opponents Alan Page and Jim Marshall by over 100 pounds. When Raider tight end Dave Casper lined up beside them, it gave the running backs a surging wall of blockers to follow. Clarence Davis ran behind these men on this important third down. They smashed such a hole in the Viking line that Davis rambled for 35 yards before he was stopped. The Raiders then drove all the way into field-goal position and took a 3-0 lead on an Errol Mann field goal.

When they weren't running over the Vikings, the Raiders burned them with long Kenny Stabler passes.

Having beaten the Vikings with their running, Oakland then went to the pass. Ken Stabler set up two touchdowns with almost identical passes to Fred Biletnikoff inside the Viking one-yard line. On the first touchdown, Dave Casper sneaked into the corner of the end zone to grab a Stabler pass. The second touchdown came on a plunge by reserve running back Pete Banaszak.

Meanwhile the Raider defense, which was not considered one of the NFL's best, had shut down the Viking attack. Minnesota seemed to have trouble with the Raiders' three-man defensive line backed up by four linebackers. Foreman, Tarkenton and the rest were shut out in the first half, and Oakland took a commanding 16-0 lead to the dressing room.

The Raiders had made no secret about their game plan. Of the 20 running plays they had tried in the first half, 17 went behind Shell and Upshaw. In the second half, the Raiders continued to pound the left side. They drove for another field goal to gain a 19-0 lead.

Late in the third quarter, the Vikings began a comeback. Despite jarring hits from safety Jack Tatum, Sammy White made some courageous catches to keep his team moving. White capped the drive by grabbing a seven-yard toss for a touchdown.

For once the Vikings held off the Raiders, and they drove again to Oakland territory. With a second and one on Oakland's 35, they seemed in good position to make it a close game. But the Raider linebackers dropped Foreman for a loss. Then tall Ted Hendricks rushed Tarkenton into throwing an interception to Willie Hall, who always seemed to be in the right spot. Then for the third time, Biletnikoff caught a long pass to set up a Raider touchdown. Banaszak plowed over to up the score at 26 to 7.

The final frustration for the Vikings came when Tarkenton tried a quick sideline toss to a receiver while deep in Oakland territory. Raider defender Willie Brown was waiting for just such a throw, and he intercepted. Although the veteran Brown was a slow runner, he had such a clear field in front of him that he chugged 75 yards for Oakland's final touchdown. A final Viking score, engineered by reserve quarterback Bob Lee, was meaningless, making the final count 32 to 14.

After years of frustration, the Raiders could finally claim the title of "Number One."

While the long-awaited victory was sweet for all of the Raiders, it was especially so for three of the Raiders' stars of the day. Pete Banaszak had scored twice, and Gene Upshaw had paved the way for Oakland running backs to pile up an incredible 266 yards rushing. Their third hero, Fred Biletnikoff, won Most Valuable Player honors for setting up three Oakland touchdowns. The three had waited almost 10 years for this victory. All three had played in the 33-14 loss in Super Bowl II and had gone through all of the other frustrating play-off losses. At last their chance for glory had come, and they had made sure it did not slip away again.

Four years later, in 1980, Oakland was working even harder to keep up its image as the misfit of pro football. Owner Davis had defied NFL rules by trying to move his team to Los Angeles without league permission. That led to court cases, charges, and countercharges between Davis and NFL Commissioner Pete Rozelle.

The Raiders' lineup, meanwhile, resembled a junk-salvaging operation. Tops on the list of rusty, unwanted players was Jim Plunkett. After playing for years behind poor pass-blockers, Plunkett had withered from a star quarterback to a timid reserve.

When even the lowly San Francisco 49ers cut him in 1978, Jim seemed washed up. For two years he did nothing but fill a spot on the Raider bench as a reserve to Ken Stabler and later to Dan Pastorini. But when Pastorini broke his leg early in the 1980 season, Plunkett was called on to lead the team.

Also starting for Oakland were linebackers Rod Martin and Bob Nelson, who had both been cut by several teams, and 12th-round draft choice Reggie Kinlaw at nose guard. At safety was Burgess Owens, a man who had been unimpressive with the New York Jets. The Raiders' top running back, Kenny King, had been salvaged from the Houston Oilers, where he had played behind the great Earl Campbell. With such a crew, football experts predicted that the Raiders would finish last in their division.

But instead Plunkett, who had enjoyed fine protection from his line, came through with key long passes. And led by Ted Hendricks and Lester Hayes, the Raider defense was even more spectacular. Hendricks, although a linebacker, played his own special position and charged into the offense wherever he was least expected. Hayes, considered a soft spot by some quarterbacks early in the year, easily led the league in pass interceptions with 14.

These performances led Oakland into the play-offs as a wild card team with an 11-5 record.

Making the play-offs was startling enough for the Oakland team. And for them to win three tough play-off games to get to the Super Bowl seemed like it would take a miracle. But as it happened, the Raiders got some extraordinary breaks.

Cleveland was well within range of a game-winning field goal in the final seconds of their game with Oakland. But instead they chose to try one more pass. Oakland's Mike Davis intercepted, giving his team a 14-12 win.

The following week, a lucky bounce gave Oakland its margin of victory over San Diego. A pass bounced off Oakland's Kenny King into the arms of tight end Ray Chester for a long touchdown in their 31-27 win.

The Raiders faced the Philadelphia Eagles in Super Bowl XV in the New Orleans Superdome on January 25, 1981. Coach Dick Vermeil had run his Eagle team through the league's most punishing workouts all year. They were a tough, determined group, led by a defense that had no weaknesses. On offense they relied on the running of Wilbert Montgomery and the passing of Ron Jaworski to 6-feet, 8-inch Harold Carmichael.

Super Bowl XV is just about to begin as Raider captain Gene Upshaw and Eagle veteran Harold Carmichael shake hands at midfield.

Rod Martin gave the Raiders a break early in the game by intercepting a pass in Eagle territory. Then Oakland found that good fortune was still on their side. First, the Raider drive was kept alive by an offsides penalty on the Eagles. Plunkett threw 2 yards to Cliff Branch for a score to complete the drive. Second, a long Eagle touchdown pass to Rodney Parker was called back because of a motion penalty on Carmichael. Third, Plunkett scrambled out of trouble, turning a messed-up play into an 80-yard touchdown pass to Kenny King. This, added to Oakland's tough defense against the run, sent them to the locker room with a 14-3 halftime lead.

In the second half, Plunkett's blockers gave him plenty of time to pick apart the Eagles' defense. He capped one drive with a 29-yard pass to Cliff

An official raises his arms to signal the first of Cliff Branch's two touchdowns for Oakland in Super Bowl XV.

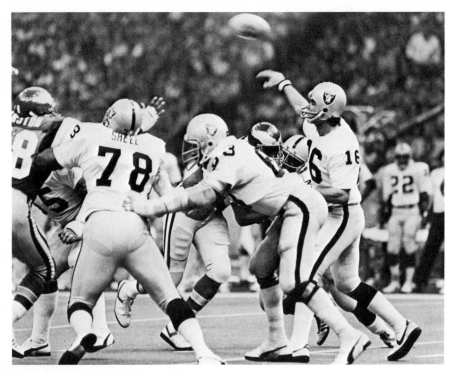
Written off by the experts as washed up, Jim Plunkett surprised the football world by leading the Raiders to the Super Bowl and then by defeating the favored Eagles, 27-10.

Branch, who stole the ball from Philadelphia's Roynell Young at the goal line. After the Eagles closed to within 11 points, Plunkett led Oakland to two field goals for a comfortable 27 to 10 lead. Even the Eagles' normally unbeatable rushing defense could not stop the powerful wall of blockers and the tough Raider runners. Meanwhile Rod Martin was finishing off the Eagles and intercepted his second and third passes of the game. Martin had a strong claim to the Most Valuable Player Award, except that this was Jim Plunkett's finest hour.

Plunkett finished the game with 13 completions in 21 attempts for 261 yards. In a year when the cast-off Raiders won the Super Bowl, it was only fitting that the chief castoff of them all, Plunkett, won the game's Most Valuable Player Award.

Raider linebacker Rod Martin holds the ball high after making his third interception in Super Bowl XV to set a Super Bowl record.

Dallas lineman Bill Gregory lands a stiff arm to the chin of Denver
center Bobby Maples in Super Bowl XII action.

3
Dallas
Cowboys
SUPER BOWL XII

The Dallas Cowboys are often said to be the most organized team in football. Their organization is so full of computer printouts and stacks of complicated information that it is hard to tell if they are running a football team or the space program. Over the past 15 years, no team has done better at inventing plays and formations and at finding good players than Dallas.

While great teams have come and gone over the years, Dallas seemed to have great teams every year. Even Super Bowl champions such as Green Bay, the New York Jets, and Kansas City fell to the bottom of the standings once their top players quit playing. After a decade of rebuilding, these teams are still struggling to get back to their old winning ways. The Cowboys, on the other hand, replaced players as easily as if they were spare parts on a machine. Dallas won two Super Bowls in seven years, and they did it with two almost entirely different teams.

By 1977, five years after their first Super Bowl win, almost all of the old Cowboy stars were gone. Only 6 of the 22 starters in Super Bowl VI were still around. Yet the Cowboys were back for their fourth Super Bowl, having lost in 1975 to Pittsburgh. Part of the credit for this amazing rebuilding job had to go to the Dallas draft of college players in 1975. No less than 12 rookies made the Dallas team that year, including defensive tackle Randy White; linebackers Bob Breunig, Thomas Henderson, and Mike Hegman; defensive back Randy Hughes; and offensive linemen Herbert Scott, Pat Donovan, and Burt Lawless.

With the development of two unstoppable defensive ends, Harvey Martin and Ed "Too Tall" Jones, Dallas quickly formed a defense just as awesome as the old Doomsday unit. And the addition of college superstar running back Tony Dorsett gave quarterback Staubach another great offensive weapon.

Tony Dorsett gave the always-powerful Cowboys something they had lacked for years—an explosive, game-breaking running back. With Dorsett in the backfield, the Dallas offense became unstoppable.

That season Dallas had crunched the Chicago Bears and the Minnesota Vikings for the NFC title, allowing the two teams a total of only 13 points. Their Super Bowl opponent in the New Orleans Superdome on January 15, 1978, was the hard-hitting Denver Bronco team. Denver's swarming linebackers had led that team to a 12-2 record and its first play-off competition in its history. Randy Gradishar, Tom Jackson, Joe Rizzo, and Bob Swenson roamed the field, shutting off both passes and runs. Defensive end Lyle Alzado and defensive backs Bill Thompson and Louis Wright joined them to form a ferocious defense. They were so good that Denver's mediocre offense usually played it safe and waited for the defense to give them a good field position. Denver had shut down the Oakland Raiders, 20-17, to win the right to face Dallas.

The Cowboys started off as if they were doing an instant replay of the 1971 "Stupor Bowl." They fumbled three times in the first quarter, once on their own one-yard line. But luckily for them, they recovered all three fumbles. This game actually would have as many turnovers as that 1971 contest, most of them due to ferocious tackling and pass rushing.

Helped by Cowboy fumbling, the Broncos threatened first when they reached the Dallas 34. But Denver's offensive line crumbled under the attack of the Cowboy defensive line. Right end Harvey Martin had been a one-man wrecking crew all year long. His 23 sacks led the league, and he had been named the NFL's top defensive player of 1977. If the Broncos stopped his rush, Cowboy tackle Randy White would break through. White was so fast and strong that his teammates called him the "Manster"—half man, half monster. On the other side of the line, 6-foot, 9-inch Too Tall Jones had

It's "light's out!" for Bronco quarterback Craig Morton as Too Tall Jones crashes him to the turf.

suddenly found his form in the play-offs. From the instant the ball was hiked, Bronco quarterback Craig Morton could feel the shadows of these three men closing in on him.

In the game, Morton had two choices: throwing the ball quickly or being slammed to the ground by the Cowboys. When he was not being sacked, his hurried throws were intercepted by Dallas. In the

Randy White and Charlie Waters grab Craig Morton as he watches one of his passes being intercepted.

first half alone, the Cowboy defense picked off 4 Bronco passes and recovered 3 Denver fumbles! Morton completed only 4 of 15 passes for 39 yards, and even some of those were then fumbled away! Only Denver's fine defense kept the score respectable at halftime, 13-0. Dallas' lone touchdown was set up when defensive back Randy Hughes intercepted a weak pass thrown by the shell-shocked

Morton. Even then it took a fourth-down touchdown run by Tony Dorsett to finally put Dallas
across the goal line.

In the second half, Denver came back with a field
goal. Then when Morton narrowly avoided throwing another interception, the Broncos inserted
Norris Weese at quarterback. Weese was not a top
passer, but at least he was quick enough to avoid
some of the Dallas pass rushers. Few quarterbacks,
however, would have had any luck against Dallas

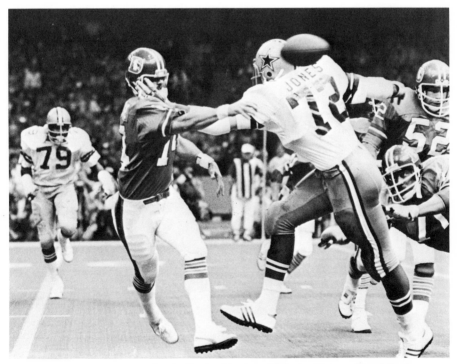

Ex-Cowboy quarterback Craig Morton had no Super Bowl luck
against his former teammates and neither did his replacement,
Norris Weese, here being smacked by Too Tall Jones.

that day. Dallas, in fact, probably would have held Denver without a touchdown if it were not for a 67-yard kickoff return by speedy Rick Upchurch. The run put Denver in position for a touchdown plunge by Rob Lytle.

Meanwhile Dallas clinched the game on two spectacular plays. On the first, ex-pole vaulter Butch Johnson made a fingertip catch while stretched out in a swan dive. The pass was good for 45 yards and a touchdown. Fullback Robert Newhouse then

Cowboy Butch Johnson stretches to haul in a touchdown pass from Roger Staubach in Super Bowl XII.

Over the outstretched arm of Denver's Steve Foley, Cowboy Golden Richards hauls in a touchdown pass from Robert Newhouse.

rolled to his left and surprised Denver by firing a perfect scoring pass to wide receiver Golden Richards. The final score: Dallas 27, Denver 10.

For the first time ever there was a tie in the voting for the game's Most Valuable Player. Randy White and Harvey Martin were voted co-winners for their tremendous pass rush, and Ed Jones could very well have been given a share in the award, too. But perhaps even more valuable were the top people in the Cowboy organization. Somehow they had retooled an old team in record time and had made it even better than it had ever been before.

49er running back Earl Cooper and end Eason Ramson slap high fives after Cooper scored San Francisco's second touchdown in Super Bowl XVI.

4
San Francisco 49ers
SUPER BOWL XVI

In 1981 the San Francisco 49ers and the Cincinnati Bengals dealt a harsh blow to the experts who boldly predict the winners of football games. No one who knew anything about the game foresaw that those two teams would play in the Super Bowl at the end of the season. Both had suffered through their usual losing seasons the year before, each winning 6 games and losing 10. Each was picked for third place or worse in their own division. But when the frost cleared from the play-off scene, it was the Bengals vs. the 49ers in Super Bowl XVI.

It was more than a matter of play-off luck that got them there. Both San Francisco, at 13-3, and Cincinnati, at 12-4, had the best records in their conferences.

Although the 49ers weren't quite the outlaws as the nearby Oakland Raiders, they, too, upset many of the rules of football. Even though there were 20 new players on the team, they played well as a team. They instantly rebuilt a defense that had been little more than an escort service for rival receivers who dashed into the 49er end zone. In 1980 the 49er defensive backs had allowed their rivals to complete two-thirds of their passes. To put a stop to that, San Francisco tried an unheard-of tactic: they put three rookies into their defensive backfield. Starting with the first exhibition game, draft choices Ronnie Lott, Eric Wright, and Carlton Williamson were rushed into action. By midseason, they were one of the top units in the league. San Francisco plugged some other defensive holes by signing Ram middle linebacker Jack Reynolds and Charger All-Pro defensive end Fred Dean.

On offense the 49ers relied on the creative genius of coach Bill Walsh. Walsh dreamed up such a grab bag of new plays that the defenses never knew what to expect from the 49ers. With such

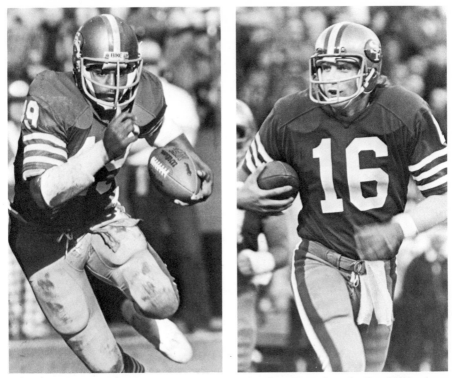
Two young athletes who blossomed for San Francisco in the 1981 season: running back Earl Cooper (left) and quarterback Joe Montana.

young stars as quarterback Joe Montana, wide receiver Dwight Clark, running back Earl Cooper, and guard Randy Cross carrying out instructions, the 49ers shocked opponents week after week. Dallas was the final NFC team to fall to the surging 49ers. In the NFC title game, Dwight Clark stretched high in the air to pull down a last-minute touchdown pass to beat the Cowboys, 28-27.

In Super Bowl XVI on January 24, 1982, the 49ers' foe was the equally surprising Cincinnati

During the 1982 AFC championship game in Cincinnati's sub-zero weather, Bengal quarterback Ken Anderson makes a handoff.

Bengals. The Bengals' new striped helmets seemed to turn the mild Cincinnati club into tigers! Quarterback Ken Anderson bounced back from being the NFL's 24th-ranked quarterback—out of 28 teams—to capture his conference's Most Valuable Player Award. With the help of Cris Collinsworth, a skinny rookie wide receiver, and enormous fullback Pete Johnson, the Bengals roared up and down the field at will. Led by linemen Ross Browner and Eddie Edwards, their defense also came alive. They held San Diego's high-scoring offense to seven points to win the AFC championship game, 27 to 7.

Fans in Detroit's Silverdome were just settling back to watch the game when disaster struck the 49ers. "Famous Amos" Lawrence fumbled the opening kickoff, and the Bengals recovered the ball at the 49er 26. But the defensive backs came to the rescue for San Francisco. Dwight Hicks, the

The spacious Silverdome, site of Super Bowl XVI, was the first stadium in a cold-weather city to hold football's showcase event.

only nonrookie in the defensive backfield, cut in front of Cincinnati's Isaac Curtis to intercept a pass on the five-yard line.

Hicks ran the ball out to the 32. It was then Montana's turn to spring Coach Walsh's clever game plan on the bewildered Bengals. The 49ers marched steadily downfield using a variety of strange formations and well-planned pass patterns, including some that had been invented only a few days earlier. Montana finished the 68-yard drive by diving over the goal line from the one.

Montana caps a 49er drive by going over the top for the score.

Cincinnati came back and again moved deep into San Francisco territory. But once more they were jolted by the 49er backs. Eric Wright stripped Collinsworth of the ball on a pass completion at the 8-yard line, and the 49ers recovered the fumble. This time San Francisco traveled 92 yards for the score, mixing up passes, runs, trick plays, and strange formations to perfection. Cooper made a fine grab of a high pass to cover the final 11 yards and make the score 14 to 0.

Cincinnati's Anderson had trouble dodging Fred Dean and the rest of the 49er pass rush, and this gave Montana another chance to move on the Bengals. Just before halftime, San Francisco drew within range of a field goal, and Ray Wersching kicked the ball perfectly to pad the lead to 17-0.

In the few seconds that remained in the half, Cincinnati managed to give away three more points. Archie Griffin and others bobbled a bouncing kick-off as if it were a wet bar of soap until the 49ers finally held on to it at the nine-yard line. Without running another play, San Francisco sent Wersching in to kick, and he made it 20 to 0.

It looked like another dull, one-sided Super Bowl until the Bengals showed up for the second half looking like a different team. Anderson moved

With Joe Montana as his holder, San Francisco kicker Ray Wersching boots one of his four Super Bowl XVI field goals. His efforts tied Don Chandler's Super Bowl II record.

them smartly downfield, gaining crucial yards with his scrambling. He finally scrambled and slid into the end zone from five yards out to close the gap to 20-7.

When the 49ers could not move against the aroused Bengal defense, Anderson led his team toward another touchdown. Pete Johnson, all 258 pounds of him, barreled for a first down at the three-yard line. Johnson then crashed into the line again, reaching the one. There was nothing fancy about the Bengals' approach, and they rammed Johnson into the line a third time. This time Reynolds stopped him for no gain. A third-down swing pass to halfback Charles Alexander looked like a sure touchdown until linebacker Don Bunz stopped him inches short with a perfect tackle. This left the Bengals with a tough fourth-down decision, and coach Forrest Gregg elected to try for the touchdown instead of the field goal. No one, least of all the 49ers, was surprised when Johnson got the ball again. They stacked him up short of the goal line and halted the Bengals' momentum.

The San Francisco line piles up Cincinnati's Pete Johnson at the goal line, stopping the big fullback cold.

In the second half, the 49ers used their running game to keep their lead. Here Bill Ring takes a handoff from Montana and follows Johnny Davis through a hole.

Although the Bengals held good field position, they did not get their second score until the fourth period. Tight end Dan Ross was enjoying a fine game, and he closed the margin to 20-14 with a four-yard touchdown catch.

Now it was time for the San Francisco offense to go back to work. This time they surprised Cincinnati by staying with their ground game. Randy Cross and Keith Fahnhorst provided the key blocks and got close enough for Wersching to kick another field goal.

It had been awhile since the 49er defensive backs had been heard from, but Eric Wright moved them back into the spotlight. He intercepted a long pass near the left sideline at the 47 and returned it to the 22. Once again Wersching's foot came through with a field goal to make it 26-14.

With the help of some more brilliant pass catching by Ross, Anderson tried gamely to rally his team. The Bengals moved downfield swiftly, scoring again on a three-yard toss to make the score 26 to 21. But by then there were only a few seconds left. When San Francisco recovered the onside kick attempt, the game was over.

As usual, a quarterback, Joe Montana, was voted the game's Most Valuable Player. He had played coolly for a third-year man, completing 14 of 22 passes for 157 yards. But it was the rebuilt 49er defense that had made the difference in the game. With five sacks, two interceptions, a fumble recovery, and a thrilling goal-line stand, San Francisco had turned back the Bengal attack. In one short season, they had turned their laughable defense into the kind that wins championships.

Super Bowl Scores

SUPER BOWL IX
January 12, 1975 / Tulane Stadium, New Orleans

Pittsburgh Steelers (AFC)	0	2	7	7	**16**
Minnesota Vikings (NFC)	0	0	0	6	**6**

Most Valuable Player Award: Franco Harris, Pittsburgh Steelers

SUPER BOWL X
January 18, 1976 / Orange Bowl, Miami

Pittsburgh Steelers (AFC)	7	0	0	14	**21**
Dallas Cowboys (NFC)	7	3	0	7	**17**

Most Valuable Player Award: Lynn Swann, Pittsburgh Steelers

SUPER BOWL XI
January 9, 1977 / Rose Bowl, Pasadena

Oakland Raiders (AFC)	0	16	3	13	**32**
Minnesota Vikings (NFC)	0	0	7	7	**14**

Most Valuable Player Award: Fred Biletnikoff, Oakland Raiders

SUPER BOWL XII
January 15, 1978 / Superdome, New Orleans

Dallas Cowboys (NFC)	10	3	7	7	**27**
Denver Broncos (AFC)	0	0	10	0	**10**

Most Valuable Player Award: (tie) Randy White & Harvey Martin, Dallas Cowboys

SUPER BOWL XIII
January 21, 1979 / Orange Bowl, Miami

Pittsburgh Steelers (AFC)	7	14	0	14	**35**
Dallas Cowboys (NFC)	7	7	3	14	**31**

Most Valuable Player Award: Terry Bradshaw, Pittsburgh Steelers

SUPER BOWL XIV
January 20, 1980 / Rose Bowl, Pasadena

Pittsburgh Steelers (AFC)	3	7	7	14	**31**
Los Angeles Rams (NFC)	7	6	6	0	**19**

Most Valuable Player Award: Terry Bradshaw, Pittsburgh Steelers

SUPER BOWL XV
January 25, 1981 / Superdome, New Orleans

Oakland Raiders (AFC)	14	0	10	3	**27**
Philadelphia Eagles (NFC)	0	3	0	7	**10**

Most Valuable Player Award: Jim Plunkett, Oakland Raiders

SUPER BOWL XVI
January 24, 1982 / Silverdome, Detroit

San Francisco 49ers (NFC)	7	13	0	6	**26**
Cincinnati Bengals (AFC)	0	0	7	14	**21**

Most Valuable Player Award: Joe Montana, San Francisco 49ers